like to introduce myself. I am
...adows (author name). I have just published my first book, Little Daisy Poetry.

...n writing poems, occasionally for a while, but during the lockdown due to Covid, I decided to write more
...'ry to encourage kindness and positivity. I joined a poetry website and received many lovely comments, so
...I to write.

...difficult times for everyone and I try to write in my poems, the importance of kindness in the world.

I would like to donate a free book and hope to spread a little joy into someone's day.

I have an Instagram account - daisymeadows2023. If you read my book, I would appreciate any feedback.
My book is available on Amazon in paperback or ebook.

Thank you for taking the time to read this.

With thanks
Daisy Meadows

# Reviews and Praise

# Poem Tributes and Acknowledgement

### Poem: Memories are priceless

A tribute to my three sons. So proud of you all!!
Thank you for bringing such joy to my life and for all the support you
have given me.
You are amazing!
You are my world.
Wishing you and your partners a bright, happy future.
Love you lots xxx

### Poem: My Mother-in-Law

A tribute to a very special lady who was a big part in my life.
Miss you very much
Love always x

### Poem: Aunty's Tomato Greenhouse

A tribute to my wonderful Aunty. Such a kind hearted lady with a calm,
gentle nature.


...and a special thank you to my Uncle, who has helped me to publish this
poetry book, giving up his spare time and to making it possible. He knows I
find technology baffling!


Best wishes,

Daisy

# Contents

Surround yourself with the people you love.

It will make your day and theirs.

# Memories are Priceless

We may not have much in life,

Or much money in our hand,

A large house or lots of land,

But our memories are priceless,

With our families we share,

Love, life and laughter,

Together with those, we care.

Our memories are precious,

And will stay with us forever,

Rich or poor,

Whatever the weather.

So treasure the special memories,

With our loved ones we share

In our hearts, you'll always be there!

Hug someone you care about.......

Just because.

# My Mother-in-Law

Women in my family -

My mother- in-law, so special,

A lady with such a kind heart,,

Always there for us,

Whether near or miles apart.

She loved the grand kids so dearly,

A special bond between them,

With deep respect clearly.

Always a smile on her face,

The laughs we all had together were ace!!!!

She always knew the words to say,

To cheer you up,

And brighten your day,

Now you are gone,

It's just not the same,

We all miss you so much,

It's such a shame,

Wish I could give you a hug,

Love you lots.

Help someone to feel special. Let them know that you are thinking of them.

# A Friendly World

Wake up in the morning,

And have a cup of tea,

Think about the world,

A better place it could be.

If everyone was calm and respectful,

A different world to see,

Friendly, caring people,

Respect and honesty.

If there was more thought on the land,

Guiding people with love,

And give a helping hand.

If everyone was kind, it would be,

Always there for each other,

A different world we would see,

Great happiness in the world,

Joy for you and me!

Kindness is free, but can make someone feel worthy.

# A Friend or Gold?

Gold, silver, diamonds and pearls,

Shining and sparkling,

Glittery when you swirl.

Dancing away,

Beautiful bright gemstones,

Brightly gleaming as you sway.

They may make you feel like magic,

Like stars in the skies,

But even without jewels,

Remember how special you are!

Loved by family and friends,

Even if near or afar.

Jewels can't show they love you,

Or when you need someone there,

Call to check your ok,

Let you know that they care!

Reminisce about your most treasured memories ....

.......Happy times.

# Close Your Eyes

If you are feeling low today,

And you are feeling grey,

Your mood is a little low,

And you don't know what to say.

Close your eyes for a minute or two,

Imagine the bright blue sky and the sun,

Shining down on you,

The breeze blowing gently,

Softly through your hair,

The warmth of the sand between your toes,

Imagine you are there!

With the sand, sea and where the sun glows,

For a minute or two,

Imagine you are where you want to be.

Feel calm and breath, imagine,

Peace and tranquillity.

Be there for each other and show you care.

Make Fond memories to share.

# World Peace

W   World Peace is needed today!

O   Only be kind and loving please!

R   Remember to be mindful in what you say,

L   Life is so short,

D   Don't waste it away,

P   Peace, tranquillity and a kind thought,

E   Every life is precious,

A   And respect is needed,

C   Consideration and don't be vicious!

E   Everyone, PLEASE BE KIND!

Kindness spreads happiness.

Spread happiness all around!

# Be Kind

Smile, be kind,

Help someone today,

Life's too short,

But memories stay!

Let's people know how special they are to you and important in your life.

## Open the Curtains

I opened the curtains this morning,

And start a brand new day,

Hope today will bring happiness for everyone,

And joy will come our way.

Spend time with loved ones,

Create some happy memories that say,

You are so very special,

And loved in every way.

If a friend is miles away,

Send a message, make them smile,

And wish them a good day.

Before you go to bed at night,

And close the curtains to,

Make sure you let your loved ones know,

They mean the world to you!!!

Be there for each other and treasure,

the special times you have together!

# Just Remember

If ever you feel lonely or down,

And your not sure what to,

Close your eyes and take a deep breath,

Remember a very happy, special day,

When things were good for you,

Remember who you were with, that special place,

That holds special memories,

Family, friends, that familiar face.

Hold on to the special memories,

Of all our loved ones, so dear,

We should treasure them forever,

Always in our hearts and in our minds so clear.

A hug can be comforting.

Give the special person in your life a hug.

# Who Knows???

Who knows what life will bring today?

Who knows what life will bring tomorrow?

Will it bring happiness?

Or will it bring sorrow?

Just want to wish you all well,

For a brighter, happier future,

Wish I could cast a spell.

Hope everything is going to be alright,

Look after each other,

From morning til night.

Wishing for a calmer world,

Hope the future is bright!

Make the most of each day.

Time is precious!

# Along Came a Flood

Along came a flood

Rushing in my head

What will today bring?

What will be said?

Will today be a sad and dull day?

Or will sunshine brighten the way?

Who knows what will happen

Nobody knows for sure

What will the future bring?

My head will roar.

Let's hope for good times,

Happiness and delight,

Let us hope that the future is bright!

Walking in the sunshine can bring a feeling of calmness and peace.

# My Dream Vacation

Stunning, amazing, outstanding view!
Bright sunny sky,
The sea such a beautiful blue.
Walking barefoot, feeling the softness of sand,
With a gentle breeze,
There's such beauty on this land.
Boats sailing,
Surfers galore,
People having fun!
I pick up shells on the shore.
Clean fresh air,
Not a car in sight,
Peaceful, calm and such a delight.
A gentle stroll along the sea,
Splashing quietly against my toes,
There's no better place to be.
Enjoy the peace and tranquillity,
It feels special,
It's for everyone to see.
We should appreciate the beauty around,
Days go so quickly,
We have all found.
For now this vacation is all in my head,
But hopefully soon, we will all be together,
It will be real instead!

Spread a little sunshine and smile!

# Magical Spell

One cup of kindness,

A spoonful of love,

Happiness, peace and cheerfulness,

And all the above.

Sparkles of magic,

Lots of group hugs,

Make things better and nothing tragic.

Mix these together,

Let the world be a kinder place,

Peace and love forever.

Planting the seeds and sow,

Remember to water them,

And patiently watch them grow!

# Aunty's Tomato Greenhouse

Walk up to the greenhouse,

Step inside the door,

There's a forest of tomato plants,

Wander around, have a look and explore.

Look left, then look right,

Then at the ceiling to the floor,

Surrounded by tomato plants,

There are tomatoes galore!

How did Aunty grow them?

Was it with lots of kindness and love?

And a watering can,

Like rain from the sky above.

Or did the fairy godmother (Aunty Phyl)

Wave her magic wand?

And sprinkle a little magic,

That made them so big and strong!

Now step outside the greenhouse,

Take a tomato or two,

They are tasty and delicious,

And also good for you!

Feel the harmony of nature,

Enjoy spending time in the garden.

# Garden Inspirations

A trowel in one hand,
Seeds in the other,
Digging the soil,
I'm a garden lover.
Doesn't matter if your garden's big or small,
Enjoying the nature,
It's good for us all!
Beautiful flowers of all colours,
Watch them grow,
Red roses and yellow crocus.
Lovely smell of fresh cut grass,
Wonderful sight of the birds flying free,
Sun shining brightly,
Through the tall leafy trees.
Breath in the fresh air,
See the beauty around,
Of the plants and wildlife show that we care.

A beautiful display of flowers in the garden,

Is such a delight to see,

A place for you to enjoy and relax,

Love the peace and tranquility!

# Just flowers

Daisies, buttercups, bluebells and trees,

Wonderful woodland,

Lots of green leaves.

Daffodils, tulips and roses,

Put them together,

Make bright coloured posies.

Carnations, lilies and orchids too,

A caring thought is sent,

Beautiful bouquet especially for you.

Flowers are special and they say,

Bringing lots of love,

To brighten up your day.

Lavender is so pretty and wonderful to see, with a lovely soothing aroma.

# Lavender

The smell of lavender is so calming,

A beautiful display of colour,

It looks so charming.

The scent often attracts the bees,

Buzzing around,

Landing gently on the leaves,

The pretty flowers they have found.

Listen to the wonderful birds singing in the morning.

A lovely start to the day!

# The Garden Visitor

Sitting in the garden,

The sun so warm and bright,

The lovely blossom flowers,

Is such a beautiful sight.

The robin happily singing,

To hear is such a delight.

He quickly swoops in,

Lands on the plate,

He knows I will feed him!

Then off to the bird-bath,

Jumps in the water,

For a quick splash,

Then he flies off again,

He does make me laugh.

He will be back again tomorrow,

And more food he will have,

So beautiful, little robin

Watching the birds in the garden can bring such joy!

# Listening to the Birds

The sound of the birds,

Is so beautiful to hear,

Day and night.

Any time of the year.

The wonderful woodpecker

Happily tapping away,

I catch a glimpse,

Before he quickly flies away.

The colourful little robin,

Is so sweet to see,

Bright colour of red,

Chirping so happily.

Chaffinch, sparrows and blackbirds,

Just to name a few,

Freedom to go where they like,

Exploring all the nature,

Then off again they flew!

Buttercups and Daisies,

A meadow with flowers everywhere,

Carefully pick one,

And place it in your hair.

# Walk Among Nature

Appreciate beautiful nature,

Flowers, birds and trees,

Bright shining sun,

Busy buzzing bees.

Nature is everywhere,

It is also free!

So go for a walk today,

And look what you can see.

Nature is all around us,

From the sky, to the ground,

Stunning colours of flowers,

Which flowers have you found?

When you go walking,

I would like to say,

Notice the nature

And have a good day!

A walk in the countryside,

With a scenic view,

Can help you stay healthy,

And is beneficial to you!

Enjoy a walk today

# A Beautiful View

Beautiful countryside,

A peaceful scene,

Rolling hills,

All covered in green.

Trees gently swaying,

In the light breeze,

Bright blue sky with clouds sailing.

High up in the air, birds fly free

Calming and tranquil,

A lovely sight to see,

Nature is wonderful,

A place of harmony.

Listening to your favourite songs,

Can brighten up your day and make you feel happy. Enjoy!

# Music and Joy

Music is like medicine
It can help you start the day.
Come on get moving,
Breath in and out,
Listen to your favourite song,
Have a dance, sing and shout.
Raise your arms in the air,
Wriggle those hips
And cheer!
Have a dance around the room,
Let's have fun,
Shake off all the gloom.
Have a fantastic day!!

Be kind to yourself and look after your body.

Healthy food choices can boost your energy levels.

Helps you to get through the day, in these hectic times.

# Healthy Living

We are what we eat,

That's what they say,

Some good old fashioned porridge,

And an apple a day.

For lunch a healthy salad,

A good start to the day,

Packed with vitamins,

And will help you on your way.

For dinner a hearty casserole,

Lots of vegetables in a stew,

Much healthier than a sausage roll,

It's good to eat healthily,

And helps to look after you!!!!

Notice your surroundings.

Look at the beautiful nature, as you go for a stroll. Wonderful!

# Healthy Choices

Oranges, strawberries, and apples too,

Containing vitamin C.

Really good to you!

Broccoli, peas and beans.

Eating healthily

Very important it seems.

Exercise also important in your day,

Walk, jog or run,

Healthy lifestyle, it's better that way,

Walk through the park, or woods in the sun

Look after yourself,

And each other,

Have fun .

It is surprising how healthy eating can contribute to feeling better in yourself.

Provides energy.

Also a little exercise can boost your mood. Worth a go!

# What shall We Eat Today

What shall I eat today?

Things that are healthy or sugary?

Banana, pasta, baked potato, one or two?

Pizza, chips, doughnuts, not good for you!

It's about balance, you know,

Healthy food, healthy heart, let's hope so.

The odd treat occasionally is OK,

Let's look after yourself, they say,

For healthy teeth, body, hair and skin,

And all the other parts within.

For more energy, healthy lifestyle,

A treat once in a while,

Eating better you will find,

You will feel better and it's good for your mind!

So be kind to yourself!!!!

The dazzling glow of the yellow sun,

Building sandcastles and eating ice-cream,

Glorious days and fun!

# Summer and Sun

Sunshine is here,

The summertime we cheer.

The warmth of the sun,

Long sunny days and fun!

Walking in the countryside,

Or going for a bike ride.

The feel of the breeze,

As you walk between the trees.

A walk by the river where the water flows,

The sun makes your skin glow.

Reflection of the swans in the water,

The ducks paddling faster.

Enjoy the summer sunshine!

The beautiful red and golden leaves,

A lovely display in the forest,

A mass of surrounding trees.

Rustling of the leaves,

Gently blowing to the ground,

Hear the crisp and crackling noises when walking,

Listen to the sound.

# Weather Forecast

Such unpredictable weather changes,

It's quite often a bit of a mix,

Will it remain calm,

Or surprise us and play tricks?

Bitter frosts on Monday,

Sunshine the next,

Rain on Sunday,

But the sunshine's the best!

Thunder storms,

Heavily the rain falls,

It is good for the lawns.

I wake up wondering,

What will today's weather be?

Beautiful sunshine the summer will bring!

A wonderful and magical scene,

Crispy, bright white snow,

Leaving a trail of footprints,

Wherever you shall go

# A Winter's Night

The stars shine brightly,

Glistening in the sky,

The darkness of the night,

Such a beautiful moon.

Gleaming, shining white, light.

Peaceful and calm, quiet no sound.

Lots of silver stars,

The frost covers the ground.

There is a chill in the air,

The scene of the night is such a delight,

A joy for all to see,

A beautiful winters night!

Even though it's cold outside,

A brisk walk can be refreshing,

Makes you come alive!

# Winter Love

Hail, sunshine, sleet and snow,

What will today's weather bring?

I don't know!

Fresh air and blustery breeze,

The rain is pouring down,

On the glistening trees.

Cool, crispy white snow,

Brightly covering the ground.

The crackling sound when walking,

The footprints of animals we found .

The sight of the robin,

Is so glorious to see.

A nice log fire inside,

And a warm cup of tea.

Christmas is a special time to celebrate with family and friends and to remember the loved ones who are no longer with us

- Always in our thoughts.

# Its Nearly Christmas

Christmas time is near,

Laughter and cheer.

Best wishes and hugs all around,

Snow glistening on the ground.

Beautiful Robins we can see,

Lots of Holly on the tree.

Time for kindness and joy,

Peace and love in the air,

Thoughtfulness everywhere.

Special thoughts for loved ones not here,

Always in our hearts throughout the year.

It's not just about the presents,

It's the love from the heart that's meant.

Special times spent together,

Happy memories forever.

Have a wonderful Christmas!

Wishing everyone a wonderful year of happiness and joy.

Be kind to each other!!!

# Happy New Year

A new year just beginning,

A good one for us all,

Peaceful,, joy and full of kindness,

If you need someone just call.

Happy times and laughter, spread,

Support each other,

Good times ahead.

Whether just quiet spells or in a crowd,

If it's calm or there's a party,

Fun is allowed!

Wishing you all happiness and cheer,

Lots of good luck and a brilliant New Year!!

Printed in Great Britain
by Amazon

36736964R00046